The Common Man

by Mark Vancil

DORRANCE
PUBLISHING CO
EST. 1920
PITTSBURGH, PENNSYLVANIA 15238

Dorrance Publishing Co
585 Alpha Drive
Suite 103
Pittsburgh, PA 15238
Visit our website at *www.dorrancebookstore.com*

ISBN: 978-1-6442-6249-8
eISBN: 978-1-6442-6431-7

Preface

The book title says it all. I am just a common man. I'm not rich, famous, or well known. I'm not a hero of any kind. I'm just another face in the crowd, just the average Joe you might see on the street on any given day. I was raised in a middle-class blue-collar home; my dad was a pipefitter welder, my mom a stay-at-home mother. My sister and I were average kids living in that setting and our family attended the Methodist church. I was brought up in the Methodist church and changed to Baptist, then Assemblies of God as time went on later in life. Sometime ago the pastor at the church my wife and I attend did a series on telling your story, what the church used to call giving your testimony. He just wanted you to give the highlights of your story so people could get the picture of what you were saying but not get bogged down in the whole story. Something like the highlights of a football game. You see the important plays and see how the game turned out and why, but you don't have to watch the whole game. I had a small issue with that, and I don't mean the word "issue" in a bad or negative way here. Looking at my life at 65, I know that anyone 50 years old or over has some stories to tell. Those stories have many highlights because we all have mountaintops and valleys in life. So my question was, how do you pick a highlight that tells everything about your life? I picked one that I put in our church publication that I'll share later in the book, but it was just one highlight or instance out of many that God has looked out for me in spite of myself. It did not tell my story completely by a long shot. I have felt for some time now that God wants me to tell my story—all of it, the good, bad, the ugly, the right and wrong. This is my first attempt to do that or write a book about it. The paths we choose to take in life have a large effect and impact on who and what we become as people and why we are the way we are.

This is the story of the paths I have taken or encountered through my life. I'm not any smarter, better, or worse than anyone else because of these paths, but they are why I am the way I am. Through it all, if I have learned anything I have learned first and foremost that God is always with me, even when it seems like he is not. I have learned not to judge others because I am not fit to do so. My halo is bent and slightly tarnished, and people who live in glass houses should not throw stones. Here, then, is my story.

Chapter 1
My Salvation

When I was 11 years old, I came across a track that church organizations put out about being saved and the way to ask for that salvation. It also had references to the consequences of not being "saved." Growing up in Sunday school, I had heard about Jesus and being saved from my sins, but something about this track made me think and look at all I had heard and read differently. I was not scared nor did I feel guilty at first, but the more I read and thought about it the more I realized that at 11 years old I had done some not-so-great or good things. It was not like I was a serial killer or had done any real "big" sin, but I had broken some of God's laws and therefore I was a sinner and needed God's forgiveness. So with an open, sincere heart, I asked his forgiveness and asked Jesus to be my Lord and Savior. Instantly the weight of the world was lifted off my shoulders. There was euphoria in my spirit that I could not explain. So in that moment I was saved, but I was to learn that salvation has to be nurtured, not just accepted, then forgotten.

Anyone who has had the salvation experience will tell you about how wonderful the experience was. At some point, however, you do get over it and life, with all its problems and temptations, goes on. Jesus in Matthew, chapter 13, verse 3, told a parable about receiving the word and then explained to his disciples what his story meant in verse 18. He was talking about all the word, so the word about salvation applies here, too. The story and its meaning is told again in Mark, chapter 4, verses 3 – 20. Any farmer will tell you that there is more to farming than just planting the seeds and letting things grow. You have to have sunlight, and depending on rain you may have to irrigate to see the plants have water. You have to keep the bugs and other pests from eating, contaminating, or just destroying the crop. In short you have to nurture the crop to ensure it grows. Likewise, with being saved your walk with the Lord does not stop once you're saved. Your salvation and walk with the Lord have to be nurtured if you're going to grow spiritually. In my life I was saved at 11, but in the teen years hormones, puberty, and porn hit me hard. Most young men and women, if not all, see or look at porn at some point. It affects different people in different ways, but it leads nowhere. It's a vicious circle seeking gratification and satisfaction where satisfaction is not found. It's also a lie; women and men are not all built like the porn stars in the movies. Love and sex are not portrayed there, just sex. A good deal of what is shown is just glorified unclean wishful thinking. The bottom line is it never satisfies; there is always another movie, another story, or another something that will give you pleasure until you need pleasure again. I am not an expert on the subject, but I'm saying I fought the porn battle for years, looking for lasting satisfaction, and never found it there. It affects other areas of your life as well, most notably your marriage, especially if your wife is a Christian or a good churchgoing woman. I have talked to people who have tried the things porn movies depict, and in most cases I was told that the swinger, threesome, and other things they tried were more harmful to their marriage or relationship than the "spice" they thought they were going find doing these things. As bad for you as porn is, what's worse is it's addictive just like a drug but in a different way. With drugs the addict is always looking for the next high, and with porn the addict is looking for the next orgasm. Only God can break the chains of porn or any other addiction, and you have to have enough faith to believe he can and will then let him do it.

Chapter 2
My Dad

I'll start by saying my dad was saved. A short time before he died, as we sat in his garage and talked he told me through tears about the day he met Jesus and got saved. I believe what he told me because while the circumstances were different for him than they were for me, his experience with Jesus mirrored my own. When God saves someone, he does not always change everything about them. There have been cases where God saved someone and lifted them out of a wheelchair and made them whole on the spot. There are times when he saved someone and left them in that wheelchair and only he knows why. JD Sumner of the Stamps Quartet once said after a discussion with a holier-than-thou Christian, "When God saves you, he doesn't necessarily change everything about you. So if you're an idiot when you're saved, then you just become a saved idiot." I am not saying or implying here that my father was an idiot—far from it. Dad was a smart man who knew what people and life were about. He was street smart in many ways, and he was one of the best pipefitter welders in the nation. I don't say that as a proud son. The fact is Dad was known in the Denver, Colorado, area and several other states where he was sent to do work for his abilities as a pipefitter. I have heard from more than one person that worked with Dad through the years about how good he was at what he did. Dad taught me the things a father should teach his son. Things like a man is only as good as his word, if a job is worth doing it's worth doing right the first time so you don't have to go back and do it again, the list goes on but you get the drift of what I'm saying here. There is a much larger list of things my dad tried to teach me, but it took experiencing life for me to find out that he knew what he was talking about. He taught me to hunt and fish and we had some good hunting trips together. Dad loved the outdoors and he loved being up in the Rocky Mountains. All this was good, but Dad had a temper that bordered on violent.

My sister speculates that Dad was bipolar and never diagnosed. He is gone now. Dementia took him about three years ago, and we will never know if he was bipolar or not. What I do know is his temper was scary. You never knew what would set him off or when he would go off. There were some things you knew would push his buttons and you avoided those things, but it was the unknown and unexpected things that kept life dicey most of the time. Once he was mad he was right, period; there was no amount of facts or any reasoning that was going to change his mind. He was right and you were wrong. Fortunately Dad was never physically abusive to me, but when he was mad and sometimes when he was not he was very verbally abusive. I was told I was useless, that I would never amount to anything; I would end up in prison or court martialed if I went into the service. Hearing these things over and over wears on you after a while. At one point, after I had done a not-real-bright thing, I don't remember what I did now, just that Dad was mad about it. I overheard him say to Mom, "Why don't you just let me knock him in the head and get it over with?" He was not joking when he said it. The bruises of verbal abuse heal slower and last longer than physical abuse, but both leave scars. I need to say here that Dad did not drink or smoke. When I sometimes get on a pity party with myself about how hard he was to live with at times, I look at the people I know who had alcoholic parents or parents that were hooked on drugs. I thank God for the dad I had. My dad never came in high or drunk and beat my mom to a bloody pulp or beat my sister or me. Mom and Dad kept a roof over our heads and food on the table. We weren't rich but we never did without the things we really needed.

Mom managed to keep some sanity around the house for my sister and me. When things got tight financially, she often did a lot with next to nothing. Mom deserves an award for dealing with Dad's temper in my youth and never losing herself in the process. Dad's temper made him very few friends; there were less than a handful in his last years. There was always a tension around the house because of Dad's temper. Even after I joined the service and was home on leave or just visiting, the tension was there, along with the temper. On one occasion, I remember Dad and I were Downtown Denver at a sporting goods store. When we left the store, Dad accidentally backed into a car parked behind him. The other driver was in his car when it happened. The bump was minimal. I don't think it even scratched the paint on either car. Dad was grumbling and upset that he could not see anything behind him in the car, which led to setting his temper off. The other driver was not upset or angry, but after about two minutes of dealing with Dad a fistfight almost erupted. If a fight had started, I wonder to this day what I would or should have done and if it would have been right or wrong. Dad's temper and my dumb stunts as a youth were a bad mix a lot of the time. When he died there, was a wall between us that he and I built together from opposite sides. It does not matter today which one of us laid the most bricks on that wall; we both share some of the blame. We got along through the years, but I think that's largely because I did not move back home after I left the military. Had I done so, there would have been things that as a teen and young man I accepted and dealt with that I would not have accepted or put up with as a grown man. We talked on the phone and saw each other every few years, but that was the extent of our contact. So in the end the wall between us kept the emotional bond a father and son should have from happening like it should have. The good news is I learned from our mistakes as father and son. My relationship with my son is many times better than what I had with my dad. I don't grieve Dad's death. In many ways it was a relief for him, I'm sure because he was very unhappy. He could not do the outdoors things he did before the dementia kept him from them. It was a relief for Mom, Sis, and me because all the tension we dealt with through the years was over. My mom bore the brunt of the tension from the time she was married to Dad till he passed. Now she is free to enjoy life more fully, without the stress she was under. While I don't grieve Dad's death, I miss talking to him sometimes. I miss hearing his wisdom on life and the interests we shared. R.I.P., Dad.

Chapter 3

Forgiveness

After the last chapter, it might seem that in some ways I have not forgiven my dad for the hurt and stress he gave me through the years. Then on the other hand, I need forgiveness for the trouble and hardships I caused him over the years. I don't read the Bible every day. I have not read the Bible cover to cover. If I read the Bible just to say I have read it, I'm really just reading words and not getting much out of it. When I'm looking for answers or trying to find something, the Bible has been a big help. The things I'm writing about here I have read in the Bible, but I'm writing about how the scriptures have applied to my life. I'll list scriptures as a reference along the way, but my point is how those scriptures have impacted my life to this point. That said, let me tell you what I have learned about forgiveness.

First, there are two kinds of offenders: those who don't know they hurt you and those who don't care. In both cases the offender goes on about their business, losing no sleep while you fume and hurt and stay upset. The person who did not know or mean to hurt you if you tell them they hurt you will most often apologize and try to make amends. There are no guarantees you will get an apology, but that type of person did not set out to hurt you to begin with, so odds are good everyone will live happily ever after. All you can do with the person who does not care is forgive them and go on your way. Odds are they meant to hurt or offend you anyway. To forgive is both Biblical and for you, not the person your forgiving. There are a multitude of scriptures that deal with forgiveness in the Bible. Most scriptures deal with Jesus forgiving someone for something that they have done, sins against God. The forgiveness I'm talking about here is found in Matthew, chapter 18, verses 21-35. There is another reference in Mark, chapter 11, verses 25 and 26. What I have learned in life is if you harbor hurt, hate, and anger, it will eventually destroy you. The person who does not care will go on with his or her life not caring you're hurt, and you will destroy yourself because of that hurt. Don't think that if you forgive someone for something they did to you that they will fall all over themselves in appreciation that you forgave them; it most likely won't happen. Memory is the biggest hindrance to forgiveness. You can forgive someone for what they have done to you, but you can't forget it happened. You have to keep in mind, only God can change a heart and that's not in your job description. Billy Graham said it best when he said, "It's God's job to judge, the Holy Spirit's job to convict, and my job to love." There are times when the hurt is so bad you can't forgive, and that's when you have to ask God's help with forgiveness.

To go back to my dad. When I think of all that God has forgiven me for and all the things I have done wrong, how can I not forgive my dad for the things he put me through? Yes, I remember the things that happened but he does not remember them now, and when we meet in heaven someday I won't remember them either. So I'll only carry the burden of memory about those things till we see each other again, and when we do we will be as a father and son should be, with no painful memories of troubles past.

Chapter 4
The US Air Force

Truth be told, my heart was with the Navy from the time I was very small till I got ready to enlist. I was in the US Naval Sea Cadet Corps from the time I was 14 till I turned 17. I'll talk more about the USNSCC in a later chapter. How then did I end up in the Air Force, you ask? It was 1972. The Viet Nam War was still raging. The military was not a popular place to be, and President Richard Nixon was about to end the draft, making the military an all-volunteer force. The recruiters panicked because their job was about to become much more challenging. The end result was if you talked to any one recruiter you were going to hear back from all of them. My heart and intent was to go Navy and be a UDT diver or a SEAL. The Navy recruiter was not telling me what I wanted to hear; hindsight being 20/20, that was more my fault than his. In the end the Air Force recruiter had what sounded like a better opportunity, so off to the Air Force I went. I enlisted December 5, 1972, and reported for active duty on January 30, 1973. I did basic training at Lackland AFB in San Antonio, TX, and went from there to Chanute AFB, Rantoul, IL, for sixteen weeks of aircraft tech school. My job and training was for what the Air Force called Aircraft Environmental Systems. This was cockpit heating and air conditioning, cabin pressure, the pilot's oxygen system, anti-ice and rain removal systems, along with a host of smaller systems like high- and low-pressure air systems that went to other parts of the aircraft. When I left tech school I was sent to Bergstrom AFB, Austin, Texas. Once I started working on aircraft, the other shops just called our shop mechanical accessories, or "MA" shop for short. Working on a multimillion-dollar jet aircraft, you learn quickly that it's imperative that you do your job right. The pilot's and aircrews' lives depend on it. Every tool you use on that airplane has to be accounted for when you're finished working on it. Your work is checked and inspected by your supervisor, and Quality Control roams the flight line at times, doing spot checks. Every nut, bolt, and washer or screw that has been replaced or changed from the time the aircraft leaves the builders' production line and enters the Air Force inventory is documented in the aircraft forms. The forms are the record of ALL maintenance done, parts changed, etc. If you looked at an aircraft only and did no work on it, you had about thirty minutes of paperwork to do when you got back to the shop. If you worked on something, you might be looking at one and a half hours of paperwork or more depending on what you did. I worked on the RF 4 C Phantom II aircraft. It was the resonance version of the F4 C model. It just took pictures and had no armament. I also worked on T29s, T39s, a KC135 midair refueler, a couple of C-118s, and other models of the F4, D, E, and one J model. Long story short, if it belonged to our military and needed to be fixed and what was broke was part of what I worked on. I fixed it.

The most sobering experience I had doing my job on the aircraft was the story I'll write about here. The ground crew was about to launch an aircraft one afternoon. The pilots were strapped in engines running and they were ready to taxi. The pilot noticed he could not get any cold air in the cockpit; the AC was not working right. Job Control called our shop and sent me out to the plane to see if I could fix the problem and get the aircraft on its way. I could not find the problem without having a large panel pulled and a ground maintenance engine run done. So they shut the engines down and got out of the aircraft so we could set things up to find out what was wrong. The pilot asked me how long it would take to fix, and I gave him a rough estimate on the time involved. It was almost shift change while we were talking and my relief showed up, so I gave him the turnover, told him what we were waiting on, then went back to the shop and home for the night. When I came in to work the next morning, I was greeted with the news that the aircraft that I looked at the day before had crashed and the pilot I had talked to the day before was dead. My first thought was, what did we do or miss here, and was this somehow my fault? As it turned out, it had nothing to do with what our shop or I did. I had not really touched the airplane; I was waiting for the ground crew to pull a panel and set up for an engine run. Second shift found and fixed the problem with the AC on the airplane, and it was cleared for flight. It was pilot errors that led to a midair collision that caused the crash. When the pilot ejected, the canopy unlocked but did not open or blow like it was supposed to. The seat and pilot were blown through the canopy, killing him instantly. Bottom line, what happened was not my fault but it got my attention, and from that point forward I did not take my job casually.

As I said earlier, the Navy and diving is what I had wanted to do all my life. I got the opportunity while I was in the Air Force to learn how to scuba dive. Under the NASDS program, I took every advanced class I could take, almost going to instructor diver. I mention this here because the next chapter deals with the next diving training I had. The training the Air Force gave me has been of great benefit to me all my working life. It has helped me in more ways than I can count, and my time there was not wasted in any way. Tech school taught me to read wiring diagrams and taught me basic electrical troubleshooting. Those things helped learning to read building blueprints and becoming an electrician later. I left the Air Force on January 28, 1977, went to a couple of semesters of collage at ACC (Austin Community College), and then on to pursue my dream of becoming a professional diver.

The McDonald Douglas RF 4C Phantom II in flight.

After completing a pre – strike photo run over the target the aircraft taxies to a stop on the flight line The film is then taken for processing & evaluation before the target is bombed.

Picture 3 Me standing in front of the left camera bay window on the nose of the aircraft. Note the camera lens behind my head.

Chapter 5
Diving School

I am often amused when I see the ads for deep-sea diving school in *Skin Diver* or *Popular Mechanics* magazines. Typically there are one or two young men in crystal-clear water in lightweight diving gear, smiling with a wrench in each fist. The ad states something like you can be a diver, too, make a lot of money, see the world, etc. The reality of the diving industry is most of the diving done is in dirty, cold, dark water, where you can't see your hand in front of your face and you have to work strictly by feel. If you're a tender or a diver tender, 90 percent of your time is spent hauling tons of diving equipment to or from a jobsite, setting it up or tearing it down, and checking, then double checking everything after setup, making sure it's all good before you put a diver in the water. If you're a diver, you're at constant risk of serious injury or possible death. You're diving in conditions mentioned above, and for the most part you can't buy even if you can afford life insurance. It's cold, hard, dangerous work that overall few people are cut out for. Most diving schools require you to be a certified scuba diver preferably with an advanced certification before they will accept you as a student. The more advanced your certification is and the more you have been taught about physics and physiology related to diving, the better off you are. You will see why that is as you read on here. To give you an idea of what you're getting into, this is the list of subjects covered in the course curriculum: Air/Mixed Gas Diving, Physics and Physiology related to diving, Diving Tables, Decompression and Treatment, Hyperbaric

Chamber, Neurological Examinations, Standard Red Cross First Aid and CPR, Diving Equipment, Applied Diving Techniques, Salvage, Rigging, Demolition, Underwater Welding and Burning, Repair and Maintenance of Diving Equipment, Diesel Engine and Air Compressor, Theory Operation and Maintenance, Offshore Commercial Diving, and Mixed Gas Diving.

The first day of diving school, the first thing they do is to try to weed out all the glory boys. Those guys who seem to think they're going to find a pirate's chest full of gold or fight a shark or wrestle an octopus. They tell you every graphic horror story about divers that have been injured or killed on a diving job that they know of. These stories are true and can with a little research be verified. This tactic works to some degree. We lost three students on the first day of school. Those of us who remained were typical young men. We were all ten feet tall, bulletproof, and stupid. Stupid in that we all thought if anything bad happened here it would happen to that other poor schmuck but not me. Then after that first day, the first week of school, the brainwork starts. You learn in basic scuba school about air embolisms. In this school you learn about Subcutaneous Emphysema, Mediastinal Emphysema, and Spontaneous Pneumothorax. They give you medical terms like Isobaric Counter Gas Diffusion, Carotid Sinus Reflex, Isobaric Ostnocroses, and a host of other terms that you are to learn and understand in a short period of time. The first week is a lot like Pre-Med but for divers, not doctors. We lost two more students because of the academics in that week. As you move into the next week of training, you start to train on the hyperbaric chamber and how to operate it. You start to learn all the diving tables you will need. These tables include the US Navy standard air decompression tables, Mixed Gas decompression tables, Surface decompression tables using air (Sur D Air), Surface decompression tables using oxygen (Sur D O2), and decompression treatment tables for different diving injuries. While all this is going on, you're also learning how to use the old-style diving suit with the breastplate and helmet, along with lightweight diving gear in the training tanks. Your instructors focus shifts at this point in your training. They are no longer just teaching classes; they are finding ways to put you under a lot of stress. They're creating any emergency they can think of to test your reaction. They are teaching you to handle emergencies with a cool head and not to panic. Examples of what I mean here: An instructor will watch and wait till everyone on the diving deck is busy or otherwise distracted, then shut off the supply valve that puts air down the divers' umbilical. The old-style diving suit and helmet, or hat, as it is called by the divers, is supposed to be dry and made of heavy canvas to protect the diver. It's cumbersome and not real easy to move in until you're in the water, and even then it's a challenge to move in at times. The air that is moved through the hat circulates at 4.5 cubic feet of air or gas per minute. The suits we had were used by so many students, they leaked badly. On any given dive, there was water in the suit up to your collarbone. You had to wear a wetsuit under the canvas suit to keep warm in the cold water. As long as air was flowing through the hat, the water stayed around your collarbone. When an instructor cut your air off, you could hear the air flow through the hat slowly and then stop. A non-return valve in the hat kept all the air in the hat from being pushed back out. That valve, if it failed for any reason, could result in the water pressure around you, forcing the air or gas in the hat back up the umbilical and crushing your body to a jelly-like pulp in the process, then forcing your crushed body up into the hat. So there you were underwater, wearing a suit you could not swim in or get out of, and you had only the air in the hat to breathe. When you took your first breath, you reduced the volume of air in the hat and the water at your collarbone filled that spot where the air had been. The water jumped from your collarbone to just under your nose in the time it took to snap your fingers. If you are prone to panic, that might push your button. I promise you. It gave me pause for a huge Maalox moment the first time it happened to me. You learned to stay very calm and breathe slowly and shallowly. In lightweight gear where you're wearing just a dry helmet or a full face mask, when they shut your air off one second you're breathing the air they're sending down the umbilical, the next second you're sucking on nothing. You don't hear the airflow slow down or stop. There is no warning, no breathing slowly or shallowly; you just don't breathe at all. It's like someone suddenly covered your nose and mouth at the same time, trying to suffocate you, or you have your head covered with a plastic bag. There will be emergencies on a diving job, and there are ways and established procedures to deal with these emergencies. We went through drills on how to handle these things time and time again till your reaction and response were automatic. The biggest thing you learned through this time was NEVER PANIC—keep a cool head. All through training while you're practicing how to handle emergencies and learning to use the equipment doing different projects underwater, you're getting classes and practical experience on other things. Underwater Welding and Burning, Demolition, Repair of Diving Equipment, and so on. On one training dive in the hyperbaric chamber that was supposed to be a simulated treatment run, we made some mistakes that could have blown my eardrums and those of another diver out. It was right after lunch one day, and the students were lining the chamber and other equipment up for a dive to sixty feet for thirty minutes in the chamber. A sensing valve on the operator controls was left closed. That valve went to a depth gauge on the operator's panel, which told him how deep the chamber was pressurized. There are two locks or chambers that make up the chamber itself, the inner and outer lock. A big "O" ring seals the hatch on both locks. The hatch itself is concaved and chamber pressure against the hatch is what holds it shut. In diving terminology, when you say you have a hatch it means the hatch has sealed and the dive is underway or the seal is broken and the dive is over. Another diver and I climbed into the chamber and moved to the inner lock, getting ready to start the dive. The student operator had another student in the outer lock to let him know if the hatch was sealed and a radio operator to talk to us in the chamber. The student in the outer lock was not up on chamber terminology, and the sensing valve I mentioned earlier was still closed. The radio operator got on the COM box and said, "Prepare to dive." I responded saying, "Roger, we're ready." The chamber operator opened the air supply valve, the hatch between the inner and outer lock that was open about a quarter-inch slammed shut with a pop, and we started to pressurize. The chamber operator saw no indication on the depth gauge that anything was happening, so he yelled at the student in the outer lock. "Do we have a hatch?" The other student yelled back, "No hatch!" so the operator kept putting air to the chamber. Meanwhile in the chamber, we were watching our depth gauge crank down rapidly. With all that air roaring through the lock, the other diver screamed in my ear, "They're going too fast!" As I watched the gauge needle pass the 60-foot mark, I screamed to him, "They're going too deep, too!" Outside the chamber, the radio operator could see through the chamber porthole that we were clearly pressurizing. Both the other diver and I were pinching our noses, clearing our ears as fast as we could. He reached up and cracked the sensing valve that had been left closed, and when he did the chamber depth gauge jumped from 0 up to 350 feet and settled back on 80 feet. At that point the chamber operator shut the supply valve off and we stopped our descent. All totaled up, it took the chamber operator thirty seconds to blow the chamber from 0 to 80 feet with two of us in the chamber. No one was hurt, but that's how divers get hurt and how fast things happen sometimes in the diving industry. This is why the training is the way it is, hard and throe.

At the end of four months, we were given our final exam. It took eight hours to take the test with no breaks, and the test covered in random order everything we had been taught from day one. They would ask what table you needed to use for a dive to a cretin depth and what decompression stops were required. A diver comes up after a dive with these symptoms, what is wrong and what treatment table do you put him on, what is the detonation rate of prima cord or det cord, how much amperage do you need for an underwater weld, what size is the cable from the welding machine to the stinger, and what's the formula for finding volume of a ship or other object that you need to float? I graduated in the top 5 percent of the class and worked for a while with Oceaneering Int. out of Morgan City, LA, and then out of Freeport, Texas.

Picture 4 Diving school A diver emerging from one of the training training tanks.

Picture 5 one of my roommates took this picture of me through an observation porthole in the training tank wall.

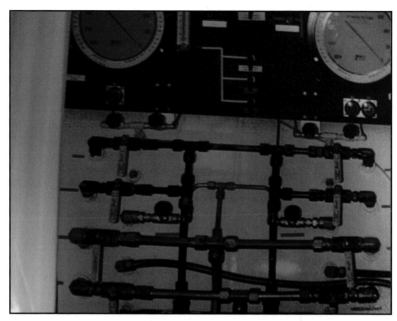

Picture 6 The control valves on the hyperbaric chamber.

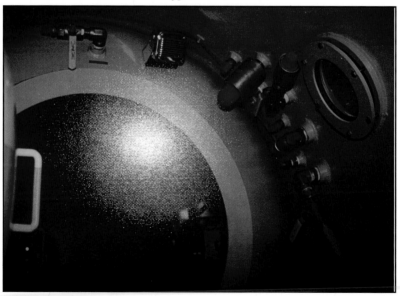

Picture 7 the outer lock of the hyperbaric chamber.Note the handle on & the curvature of the hatch to the left of the picture. The valve over the hatch is a crossover valve to equalize pressure between the inner & outer locks. The silver box over the hatch is one of the com boxes for communication with the surface crew.

Picture 8 The controls on the inner lock & controls on the lock wall.

Chapter 6
The Offshore Oilfield

Anyone who has worked on an offshore oilrig will tell you it's a dangerous place to work. You don't have to do anything wrong other than be in the wrong place at the wrong time and someone else's mistake can get you hurt or killed. The rig itself is pretty much a floating time bomb with chemicals aboard that if mixed wrong can be deadly or explosive. Then there is the well. A number of things can happen there, including a blowout or control loss of the well, and the list goes on. You have to have your head on a swivel from the time you leave your stateroom till you leave any of the decks on the rig. A diver deals with all that in addition to all the other hazards he faces doing his job. I was only in the Gulf of Mexico on a few oilrigs for a short time before I decided to leave the diving industry. My first reason was in two months I had two rigs where a problem was caught before any real bad damage could be done. Had these problems not been caught, the rigs could well have been blown out from under us. There are a lot of close calls on the Gulf rigs that you never hear about, not to mention workers injured and sometimes killed.

The last job I was on in the Gulf was the one that made me look at a career change. An oil company, who I will not name, had a blowout on the well and shut the BOP (Blow-Out Preventer) stack down, then pulled the marine riser off the equipment on the Gulf floor. By way of explanation here, if you did not understand that last sentence, the movie *Deep Water Horizon* shows what a blowout is. The movie is based on a true story about the oilrig *Deep Water*

Horizon, which had a blowout and sank in the Gulf of Mexico. All blowouts do not all happen the way the *Deep Water Horizon* happened. There are many things that can cause a blowout. The BOP stack that sits on the Gulf floor has two control lines, one called the choke and one called the kill line, that "mud" (chemicals from the rig mixed to control wellhead pressure) is circulated through. In the stack are three rams or valves designed to shut the well down if the rig loses control of it: the Blind ram, the Pipe ram, and the Shear ram. These rams are able to shut the well down and cut the drill pipe off if need be. In the movie and on the real *Deep Water Horizon*, the stack failed for a number of reasons and the entire rig was lost as a result. Now back to my last job in the Gulf. There had been a blowout. The rams on the stack were closed and the well shut down. The marine riser (the pipe that comes off the top of the BOP stack), which the drill pipe and drill bit goes through), was pulled off the stack and the stack left on the sea floor. The unnamed company was concerned a fisherman might catch his nets on the stack about three hundred feet down on the sea floor and a lawsuit would be filed. Another rig was sent to the site to find and cap the well, then retrieve the BOP stack. I was on a workboat that was loaded with about two tons of diving equipment for the job. We left Homa, LA, went down the Mississippi River to the Gulf of Mexico, and by the next day we were eighty miles off Port Aransas, Texas, shore. We loaded all the equipment onto the rig and then went aboard the rig ourselves. There was concern that the well was leaking hydrogen sulfide gas. So there was no welding on deck and no smoking anywhere on the rig. There was someone on deck taking air samples every thirty minutes to make sure the air was safe to breathe. We were all trained in the use of Scott air packs, which had been placed aboard the rig just in case they were needed. We put a remote TV camera in the water to find the stack, and once it had been found we put four divers in saturation at three hundred feet to clean and reconnect the hydraulic lines to the stack. Quick note here: Decompression in diving is determined by how deep you have been and how long you have been there. In saturation diving, you are held at your working depth till your body tissues are saturated with the gas you're breathing (nitrogen or helium air or mixed gas). That way your decompression time does not vary or change and you can decompress at a fixed rate. Once our divers had cleaned the stack off and reconnected the hydraulic lines, the crew rig opened the rams on the stack and had our divers disconnect the hydraulic lines. Then they started to drill again. Now we were sitting on a live hole with no way to close those rams again if anything happened. At any time during the day, you could see bubbles coming up off the stack to the surface. The assumption was those bubbles were the hydrogen sulfide gas they were concerned about. Then at about 1:30 in the morning, I was standing in the saturation control room talking with another diver and a bell tech when I looked out the door over the moon pool at the bottom of the rig, and the water, which should have been black at that hour of the morning, was as white as typing paper. Huge gas bubbles were exploding onto the surface of the water. They had hit a large gas pocket drilling, and now a large amount of gas was forming a big bubble under one of the caissons the rig was built on and we started to lose lift on that caisson. The rig listed about 10 degrees to the port side, but before we capsized ballast control caught up with the problem and made the rig right again. Then they put out the word, no more drilling till dawn. I thought that order was given so the Coast Guard could see where the survivors were, if there were any to find. A large tugboat was hooked up to the rig with a line, so if there was a problem like the one we had we could be pulled of the well. That tug was hooked up to us before we had the problem, and he had no clue anything had just happened.

They sent all nonessential people back to the shore the next day, and I was in that group and plenty happy to be in that group. When we got back on shore, we took a bus from the dock to the shop. The bus driver was drunk, and as one of the guys put it the whole trip back to the shop was nip and tuck the whole way. It was at that point at the age of 27 that I thought if I wanted to live to be 28 I might want to consider a career change. That was when I left the diving industry and went into the electrical trade. I would still sport dive for many years after that, but no more deep-sea diving for this cowboy. I had enough.

Chapter 7
Overconfident

When you have had the training and experience in a field like diving I have had, it's easy to forget some things and get a little cocky about yourself. That overconfidence almost killed me. I forgot that I had been told there are old divers and there are bold divers but there are no old bold divers. During one of my NASDS classes for scuba diving, the class was conducted in the Comal River in a little town south of Austin called New Braunsville. The class was for swift water and night diving. The area of the river we were in was just north of a power plant and next to a golf course. Just down from where we were located, there was a dam with three floodgates in it and a tube chute down the side. The water was crystal clear and eighteen feet deep in the deepest part of the river in that spot. Our instructor warned us about the dam and floodgates. He told us they could and would pull a diver through them. He knew because it had happened to him. Skip forward a few years, I was diving in the same spot with a friend. I remembered the warning about the floodgates I had heard way back when, but I was a highly trained diver taught by the best people in the world at what they did. I was a good student and a great diver with many underwater hours of experience, so I really did not need or heed his warning. We dropped to the bottom at eighteen feet and swam into the current, then let it carry us back downstream, then into the current again. Each time we let the current carry us back downstream, we got a little closer to the dam and floodgates. Finally we were at the dam swimming along the bottom. That was when I looked up and saw a huge gaping hole in front of me just to my left. One of the floodgates was open partway, and water was moving through it rapidly. I realized my mistake too late. Before I could react or stop myself, the current whipped my body around and I found myself wedged in the gate up to my chest. My first reaction was surprise, and I almost panicked even though I had been trained never to do that. Once I got control of myself, I started assessing my situation and options. It was during this process that I asked myself the dumbest question I have ever asked in my life: "I wonder if I should pray now." It did not take a great deal of personal debate to decide prayer was the right thing to do at that time. I promised God anything he wanted, along with things I did not even have or own. The diver who was with me was not stuck in the hole because I was plugging it up. He was trying to pull me back out of the gate. There was a steel cable stretched above us that he was hanging onto with one hand, and with the other hand he had my twin tank manifold in his grip, trying to pull me free. We had no luck and so I looked at my options again. The water here was only twelve feet deep, and with the twin tanks I had on my back there was enough air to last three or four hours at that depth if I did not do anything else stupid. You're taught never to ditch your gear unless it is hopelessly tangled in something and you can't get it free. I knew I was going down the spillway on the other side of the gate because I was not going to be able to overcome the current and get back out the way I got in here. So having my gear with me was the way to go down that spillway if I could figure out how to get unstuck. Then I noticed the gate was open just far enough that my twin tanks were what was holding me there. If I shifted my weight, I could turn the tanks enough to clear the gate and the current would do the rest, pushing me on through the gate. I shifted my weight. The tanks turned and I caught my emergency release on the tank pack on the gate. I was blown out of my tank pack and found myself hung on the outside of the dam with my tank pack pinning one side of my elbow to the inside of the dam. Water was rushing past my face, and I was about to lose my regulator and facemask. I took one last drag off my regulator, then spit it out. I wrenched my elbow free and did about three front summersaults down the spillway. When I stopped, the current was still running over me and I could not sit up into it. I rolled to my left, and the current rolled me twice more before I got my feet under me and was in waist-deep water. My gear had come through the gate behind me and was floating next to me. Mike, the other diver, managed to crawl out of the current in full gear and said to me later it seemed like an eternity he called me before I answered him. He said he saw me stuck in that gate and then in an instant I was gone. It scared him enough that he managed to get out of the water with his gear and the current fighting him the whole time. I lost one swim fin, some webbing out of my tank pack, bruised some ribs, and took a little skin off the inside of my left elbow. Other than that, I was unharmed. The same pride that got me into that mess would have me say here it was my training and ability as a diver and my equipment that was the best money could buy at that time that got me through the day here. The truth is God looks out for drunks, fools, little people, and guys like me. I asked his help that day, and he answered and said yes. It was not my time to die that day. If not for him, I would not be writing this story now. I get the credit here for letting arrogance and pride get me into a mess I should not have gotten into in the first place. God gets the credit for getting me through it alive.

Chapter 8
My First Commandment of Life

It would be fair to say that both my time in the Air Force working on aircraft and my time in the diving industry working offshore on oilrigs were both high-stress jobs sometimes. There were times when decisions had to be made or actions taken that had the potential of causing injury or death if a mistake was made. I'm not trying to be melodramatic about that, just honest. Both these jobs had a huge and profound impact on how I look at life and what I feel is important and not important in life. It is because I have had jobs that were sometimes really life-and-death critical that I learned not to make a lot out of nothing. My first commandment of life became and is to this day: "Thou shalt not sweat the small stuff." There are times and circumstances in life that need to be addressed in a serious manner and given the attention they require. Even so not every day is a life-or-death crisis and should not be treated like it is. Loosen up and live a little, deal with things in the manner they need to be dealt with, and don't go overboard making a mountain out of a molehill. There are some people that are not happy if there is not drama or stress or problems in their life. If these things are not present in their life, they will go out of their way to create drama or stress or problems and make themselves and everyone around them miserable. This just so they can be happy. They end up with strokes, heart attacks, and ulcers, for what, to be happy? Happy and stressed are a contradiction in terms. It's not a contradiction worth dying for.

Chapter 9
The USNSCC

The USNSCC stands for the US Naval Sea Cadet Corps. This is the training program for the Navy I mentioned early in the book. If you Google the USNSCC, you will find a plethora of information about it, the training available, what the program is set up to do, closest unit to you, how to join, etc. The "Sea Cadets" for short is a training program for the Navy that does in a slightly different way what the Civil Air Patrol does for the Air Force. The biggest difference in the programs is everyone has heard about the CAP and not as many people know about the Sea Cadets or that they even exist. We used to joke that the Sea Cadet program was the best-kept secret in the US Navy. The program was federally chartered by Congress in 1962 and has been supported to the extent possible (it takes a back seat to the Navy's mission) by the Navy since it started. The Sea Cadets have become much better known today, but there are still a lot of people who do not know about the program. Since my goal as a young man was to join the Navy, I was a Sea Cadet for four years in my teens. In 1987, years later, a unit was being formed in Austin. I heard about it and joined as a volunteer. I am what is called a plank owner because I was there when the unit was formed and I had a hand in that formation. I served with the Wm B Travis unit for fifteen years as an officer in the unit and held the billets of Asst. Training Officer, Operations Officer, Executive Officer, and Recruiting Officer. When people would ask me about the program years ago, there were two questions they would always ask and they always asked the questions in this order. Question 1: Does the Navy pay you for this? Answer: No, it cost me for my uniforms, for travel and lodging, for food, and other out-of-pocket expenses along the way. Question 2: Then why do you do it? Answer: Years ago when asked that question, I would say I know what the program did for me as a young man and the things it taught me, and now it was my turn to give back. Today if you asked me that question, I would tell you that for fifteen years I had the opportunity and privilege of watching young men and women grow up in front of my eyes and become good, productive citizens. I can't put a price tag on that. It was one of the most rewarding experiences of my life, and I would do it all again in a heartbeat. Here are just a few of the success stories that came through our unit. Two former cadets are now Navy SEALS, one of them a Senior Chief Petty Officer. One former cadet was accepted to the Naval Academy, graduated from the Academy, and now flies choppers for the Navy. Two former cadets are police officers now, one a Sergeant, the other a Lieutenant, in different departments in different cities. One former cadet is an attorney today in Austin. The list goes on, but my point is I had a hand in all those success stories, along with many others, and it makes me glad to know I was a small part of their success.

Chapter 10

Amy

My wife and I had been married about seven years, our daughter Faith was about three and a half years old, and Sharon was five and a half months pregnant with our second child. I came home from work one night and Sharon, at that stage of her pregnancy for unknown reasons, went into labor. I rushed her to the hospital, and while I was downstairs filling out insurance paperwork Sharon gave birth to a 1-pound, 1-ounce baby girl. We named her Amy. Amy was so small, I could literally have held her entire body in the palm of my hand. The gynecologist told me Sharon was fine, but Amy was so underdeveloped internally that if she lived we were most likely looking at a short life and her medical expenses along the way would be very costly. About an hour later, the pediatrician came in and told me much the same thing and then added, "I'm concerned that the respirator we have her hooked up to even on its lowest setting may blow her lungs out. She is so underdeveloped internally." Then he asked me, "How hard do you want us to fight this if it goes bad, and I'm pretty sure it will at some point?" I told him to do what he could SHORT of pulling the plug and we would deal with whatever happened. Then seventeen and a half hours later, Amy's tiny heart could not keep up with all the medical equipment she was hooked up to and she passed from here into heaven. Looking back, I did not handle Amy's death as I should have. I was not sure how to handle everything we were going through at the time, and my reaction to all of it was to keep Sharon at arm's length, to distance myself from her and all that was happening. I was not in the hospital when Amy died. I don't know or remember where I was or why, but I was not there. Sharon felt like the one time she really needed me I was not there for her. That anger turned to a very deep hurt for a short time, and I found myself dealing with the loss of our daughter and Sharon's anger at the same time. I reached a point where I looked at our life together and the anger and hurt I was dealing with and almost decided to file for divorce. About the time I was thinking about that, Sharon was rethinking things and trying to make amends. The problem was now I was the one who was mad and not trying to get along. At some point, Sharon reached the same place I was about calling it quits. Just as that happened, I was now rethinking the whole marriage thing and thought we ought to try again. We as a couple went back and forth like that for the next nine years. It was a rollercoaster ride we both could have done without. At some point, we figured out that if our marriage was going to work we needed to work together toward the same goal at the same time. Working on that goal separately and staggered was not going to work. I'll pause this story here. The next chapter deals with the rest of the story.

Chapter 11
The Things People Say

Often at funerals, in trying to comfort family and friends you hear things like he/she lived a good life, or he is in a better place now, or you will see him again someday. We say these things because we want to comfort others in their loss. We don't, however, really think about what we're saying or the truth of what we're saying when we say it. Many years after our daughter Amy's death, Sharon's dad was on his way into eternity. Jim had been sick off and on for several years. He had a lot of physical problems in his last few years. In spite of that, I think he outlived his doctors' expectations by about four years. He was a tough old Irishman who was not too timid about telling you what he thought or how to do any given job; there was a right way, a wrong way, and Jim's way. I don't know if he overheard the doctors talking or had a vision of some sort or if he was just tired of the fight, but I do know that he knew his time here was coming to a close. He called my wife at work from his hospital room one day and told Sharon, "I'm about to go home." Sharon said, "You're going home from the hospital?" "No," he said, "I'm going home." Jim did not talk about it a lot, but he was a forgiven child of God and he knew Jesus. Three days later, he went through eternity's door like he knew he was about to. It happened at around 9:30 in the morning. Sharon called me at work and told me he was gone. I left work and went to the hospital room where the family was gathered and sat next to Jim, thinking about all the times, both good and bad, we had seen through the years. Then like a lightning bolt out of the blue, a thought hit me—Jim just met Amy, he just met his granddaughter. In that moment, all those things we say to comfort family and friends when they lose someone they care about had a whole new meaning to me. The truth of those things we say comforted me. The world thinks we believers are nuts; they don't understand what faith and hope are about and they never will. They accuse us of using our faith as a crutch. Well, guess what—that's what a crutch is for. It helps you walk when you're injured until you can walk on your own. That's what God has done for me more than once, and while I don't think of him as a crutch, if that's what you want to call him that's fine with me, 'cause he holds me up till I can walk on my own.

Chapter 12

Marriage

Sharon and I have been married for 43, almost 44, years at this writing. It has been a bumpy 43 years at times, and you have read about a couple of those bumps here. Sadly today marriage is more a temporary thing than a lifetime commitment in a lot of marriages. I say that and not mocking what God intends a marriage to be, I would also say that only in Shangri-La do things work out like they should all the time. In real life, what do you do with the husband who beats his wife and children? What do you tell the wife, marriage is a lifetime commitment, stay with a man who beats you? There are legitimate reasons for separation and divorce. The Bible says so. I do not consider myself an expert on anything, much less marriage. A coworker once asked me when he found out how long I had been married, "What's the secret to a good marriage?" I'll repeat here what I told him. First there are no secrets. A comedian once said, "Love is blind, but marriage is an eye opener." You only think you know someone till you live with him or her. After enough time together, all the secrets, skeletons, dirty habits, and everything else you don't really want the other person to know come out in the light. After a period of time, you don't even have to say there is something wrong; your spouse can sense it by the way you look or act. Don't try to keep any secrets from your spouse. Bottom line, you and Victoria have no secrets in marriage. Next you have to be willing to accept each other's faults unconditionally. You both have them, and marrying him or her will not change that. Don't think that your love will change someone—it won't. If he or she is not willing to change, it will not happen no matter how much you love him or her. Only God can change a heart and cause someone to change himself or herself. If you can't be accepting and tolerant of each other's faults, then don't get married. Remember, while you're marrying him or her, their family is part of the package and if you can't deal with them before you get married, odds are it's not going to happen after you're married. Work on common goals together at the same time; teamwork is better than going it alone. These things are not all there is to know and do in a marriage, but it's a good start.

Let me share a couple of married stories here. One story is about Sharon and me, the other is about kids in marriage (kids tend to happen when you have been together a while). Years ago our church had a theater ministry; we are talking about armatures putting on full-blown professional-quality productions. Because of some of the training I have had along the way, I handled all the special effects on stage. If it burned, smoked, fogged, or blew up, I was the guy they called to make that happen. Sharon took care of the props backstage. One night during a dress rehearsal for a show, Sharon was carrying some props down some stairs and twisted her ankle. The news of what had happened went out on all the crew headsets, and when I knew it was Sharon that was hurt I shut down the effects board and made my way to where she was. As I reached the spot, there was a large group of women standing around Sharon, praying for her. Just as I got there, one of the women turned around and I asked her if Sharon was okay. She thought about that for two or three seconds and said, "I don't know, does she have a high tolerance for pain?" I thought about that for two or three seconds and said, "Well, she has been married to me for over 25 years. I think that qualifies." Story 2: When our son Eric was in kindergarten, I got a note from the school one day wanting me to send them a dollar for a spoon that had been bent or broken during a fight in the cafeteria. Eric knew that I did not want him fighting, but I had taught him not to put up with bullying either. Not knowing what had happened here, I asked Eric what went on that led to the fight. Eric said nothing and for the next thirty minutes or so, I continued to grill him about what had happened. Did he hit the other boy, or did the other boy hit him? Did one of them say something to the other that started the trouble, and so on. Then Eric looked me in the eyes, sighed, and said, "I don't know, Dad, it's been a long day." My last thought in this chapter: Marriage is largely what the two of you make it. If you make it good and keep God in the center of it, it will last for a lifetime.

Chapter 13
What Meanest All This

As I said in the preface, I am just a common man. I'm not any better or worse than anyone else. I hope what I have written here shows that. I did not write about my whole life here, but I did write about the most significant events that I have experienced. I have shared things I have learned through life here. I hope sharing those things will help others see you're not all alone in your trials, troubles, and questions about it all. I have had some bumps along the way, and I have made my share of mistakes. I am not perfect and I'm not fit to judge others, so I don't. Through it all, God has looked out for me. If you ask me why, I don't know. Every bump and scrape I have been through that I have written about here, he was with me. I might not have acknowledged that as I wrote about it, but he was there then and that's why I'm here now. I have the same questions everybody else has. What have I done during my life that really made a difference? Have I helped anyone else on their way through life? If I were God, what would I do with a kid like me? I have done things I know God would not smile on, and I have sometimes done those things knowing God would not approve. How much have I done for God in my life and was it enough, was he pleased with it? Did I do it all for me to feed my ego? At what point does God say enough is enough and punish me for the wrong things I have done? Especially those things that I knew when I did them they were wrong and God did not approve? If you have those questions, too, then you're in good company with me. I have questions about all this that I don't have the answers for right now. This I do know: God has never abandoned me or left me alone. He has watched over me and protected me more times than I can count, and I have no idea how many times he has watched over me and protected me that I don't know about. My message here is if he will do it for me in spite of who and what I am, he will do it for you. All you have to do is ask him to forgive your sins and let Jesus into your life with an open, honest heart. That's the one prayer God will NEVER say no to. He is willing to forgive you if you're willing to let him and be forgiven. Only you can make that decision and pray that prayer. No one can make the decision for you or ask God to save you from your sins—that's all on you. In many ways, the salvation prayer sounds too simple to be true, but it is true and it is just that simple.

I'm done here. I have written what I wanted to share, and it is my sincere hope and prayer that it touches or helps someone else along their way in life.